W9-AYL-330

SASTER

THE MOUNT ST. HELENS VOLCANO

WILLIAM BANKIER

Artesian **Press**

P.O. Box 355 Buena Park, CA 90621

Take Ten Books
Disaster

Other Take Ten Themes:

Mystery
Sports
Adventure
Chillers
Thrillers
Romance
Horror
Fantasy

Project Editor: Dwayne Epstein
Assistant Editor: Molly Mraz
Graphic Design: Tony Amaro
Cover photo courtesy of USGS/Cascades Volcano Observatory
©2003 Artesian Press

www.artesianpress.com

Artesian Press   ISBN 1-58659-023-5

CONTENTS

Chapter 1

Harry Truman was a tough old man of eighty-four years. He had seen everything there was to see.

He ran the Spirit Lake Lodge, a small hotel near Spirit Lake on Mount St. Helens. Mount St. Helens, one of fifteen volcanoes in the Cascade chain, is in Washington state in the northwest United States.

Tourists liked Truman a lot, and not just because he had the same name as the former U.S. President. Many people came to stay with him. "May I take your picture, Harry?" some of them would ask.

"Sure, go ahead." Harry would smile and wave his hand. He looked good standing there in front of the lodge. It is hard to say how many people have photographs of Harry Truman.

In March 1980, there were many small earthquakes on the mountain. People noticed, but nobody worried too much. In this area, tremors happened from time to time. But Mount St. Helens had been pretty quiet for 123 years.

It was not always that way. There was a big eruption in 1835. Hunters in the area wrote about it. Another happened about the time Columbus discovered America.

Scientists can pin down the time by studying lava, the hot rock that flows from a volcano. When the lava hardens, scientists can tell how old it is. With that, they determine the exact date of the eruption.

On Thursday, March 27, 1980, a small eruption took place. A depression around the opening of the volcano, called a crater, opened up on the north side of the mountain. It was the size of a football field. Steam blasted out into the air, and a black cloud rose up and dropped ash on the slopes.

This event concerned many people who lived near the mountain. Some of them made plans to leave. Valuable belongings were stored away. But Harry Truman did not prepare.

"Business as usual," he said. "It will all quiet down. We'll be fishing again in Spirit Lake just like we always did."

Chapter 2

On Sunday, March 30, 250 airplanes flew over the mountain. As long as there was daylight, the flights went on. The planes carried scientists, as well as reporters from newspapers and television. These people all felt something big was going to happen, and they wanted to be there to see it.

More news media crews drove in from many different places. It was a busy weekend. Mount St. Helens was the focus of attention.

Harry Truman watched all of the activity. Maybe he thought it would be good for business. But apart from that, it did not mean much to him.

Harry liked to tell stories to the

Harry Truman, 84, talks to visitors about his long life at the Spirit Lodge.

visitors at Spirit Lake Lodge. He spoke of the Indian legends about the volcano. Once the Great Spirit took away the sun. The tribes had no fire; they were cold. So they prayed that the Great Spirit would give them fire.

One night, the Great Spirit went to an old woman who had fire in her lodge. He asked her to make a deal. If she would share her fire, the Great Spirit said he would grant her one wish.

The old woman shared her fire. Her wish was granted; she became young and beautiful. But that was not the end of the problem. Far from it—in fact, it was the beginning of the real trouble.

The woman was so lovely that the men of all the tribes fought over her. This led to some big battles. Many of the youngest and strongest men were killed.

All of the fighting made the Great Spirit angry. So he turned two of the Indian Chiefs and the beautiful Indian girl into mountains. She became Mount St. Helens. One of those chiefs turned into Mount Hood. The other became Mount Adams.

As Harry Truman watched the airplanes fly over, one after the other, he said, "I never saw so many all at one time." They flew over all that day. They were like big, noisy birds polluting the air above his mountain. There seemed to be no end to the commotion. He would be glad when they went away.

But that was not to happen. A few days later, a larger eruption took place, and the worst was yet to come.

Chapter 3

On April 10, 1980, everyone's mood changed. First, there was a puff of white vapor. Sightseers looked up. Within five minutes, it grew into a white plume. It did not look like much, but it kept on rising until it reached one thousand feet above the top of the mountain.

Jets of black rock began to shoot out a few seconds apart. Darker clouds rolled up. A thick curtain of ash fell out of the cloud onto the slopes. Everyone there could sense danger.

Scientists began to warn people to get off the mountain. It was a serious warning. They could not say exactly when the big event would take place,

Steam rises from Mount St. Helens. Volcanoes release huge amounts of steam right before a volcanic eruption.

13

but they knew it was coming. The time to leave was right now.

Tourists paid attention to what they were being told. They quickly packed their campers and drove away. Gear was thrown inside carelessly, doors were slammed, and cars sped away.

At the same time, other men came to Mount St. Helens. They were not tourists; they were observers. They came to watch, take pictures, and keep a record of what was going to happen. To do this, the men had to get close to the action.

Reid Blackburn was an observer at the campsite called Coldwater One. He was about seven miles away from where the eruption was taking place. Gary Martin took up his position on a ridge northeast of that camp. David Johnston was located at a campsite called Coldwater Two.

All three of these men had put themselves in danger. They knew what they could expect. But as scientific observers, they felt they were in the right place at the right time. It was their chance to watch something most of us will never see.

They did not really know just how big this explosion was going to be. They knew all about volcanoes. But who could say for sure what was going to happen to Mount St. Helens?

Harry Truman did not know either, but he felt certain it would all blow over. He watched the tourists drive away. This was no big deal. He figured he would see plenty more visitors in the months and years ahead.

Harry went about his business. But as he did so, the ground continued to shake.

Chapter 4

The newspaper and television reporters were investigating the area. They found out about Harry Truman, and they spread the word. People learned that this old man was staying at his lodge far up the slope, near Spirit Lake.

A lot of people could hardly believe it. It did not make much sense. It seemed crazy for a man to put himself in so much danger. But it was true.

After hearing about Harry Truman on television, students wrote letters to him. They begged him to get away while there was still time. They worried about his safety.

Harry was glad to get the letters. He

read every one of them. He liked to read that people were thinking about him, but he did not intend to leave Mount St. Helens. He belonged on the mountain.

In late April, the steam eruptions almost stopped. The earth tremors eased off, too. Was this the end of the crisis? It seemed that Harry was right. Perhaps the old man would have the last laugh.

But the scientists on the scene knew better. People who understood volcanoes realized what this was. It was only the quiet before the storm. A last warning was sent out to leave, right now!

But it was too late for Harry Truman. He decided to stay, and he would not change his mind. He said what was really in his heart: "That mountain and that lake is a part of Truman. And I am a part of it."

Chapter 5

At 8:30 a.m., on Sunday, May 18, 1980, a blast shook Mount St. Helens. It was larger than anybody expected. In fact, this was the real thing, and its effects would be seen and felt all around the world.

The volcano sent one and a half cubic miles of material 65,000 feet into the sky. One-seventh of the mountain's height was blown away. Even in Vancouver, Canada, the smoke plume could be seen rising into the air. Can you imagine how people felt about that?

The sky was full of ash from the volcano. Some of it went as far as Denver, Colorado, a thousand miles away. In the cities of Yakima and Spokane in Washington, the huge cloud turned day into night. It felt as if the world was coming to an end.

Reid Blackburn, the observer at campsite Coldwater One, was killed. He was seven miles away, but he still was not safe. Gary Martin died, too, on his ridge northeast of that camp. Gary's last words over the radio were, "You wouldn't believe it! You wouldn't believe it!"

David Johnston, who was at the campsite called Coldwater Two, only had time to report, "Vancouver, Vancouver, this is it!" Then there was nothing but silence over the radio.

Days later, searchers would find Blackburn's sedan. Its windows were shattered, and the car was filled with ash. He must have seen the blast coming and ran to hide in his car, where he died.

As for Harry Truman, nobody knows

what happened to him. But his chances were not good. The Spirit Lake area was being swept by flows of lava. The whole area was covered by clouds of dark smoke and ash.

In such a terrible situation, where could he go? With things happening so fast, how could he survive?

Spirit Lake was boiling at this time. That water was being heated by tons of lava flowing into it. Steam in the air mixed with the clouds of ash.

The sky was darkened by ash so that the day was as dark as the night. The ash spread across the states of Washington and Idaho, and as far as western Montana.

People all over the world were interested in this exploding mountain in the northwest corner of the United States. This was a major volcano. Its power was awesome. People from all over wanted to know what was going on.

The Toutle River was jammed with logs and mud. The logs had been cut by forest workers. These men stored the logs by the bank of the river. Part of their job was to send the logs down the river in bunches. But the mud came rushing past and swept everything downstream.

The explosion knocked thousands of trees flat. All of them could be seen lying in the same direction. Their branches were stripped off. The ends of the trees were sharpened to needle points. It was as if hundreds of men had been cutting trees for weeks. But this damage was done in seconds.

The flowing mud could not be stopped. It was mixed with tons of ice blown from the top of the mountain. The mud filled the valley around the river to a depth of one hundred feet.

The volcano did terrible things to wildlife. To many people, this was the worst effect of the eruption. The animals had no warning and no time to escape. Many were destroyed instantly. Millions of fish died. The water in the rivers and lakes got so hot, fish were seen jumping out onto the shore.

And above it all, the giant black cloud hung in the sky like some evil spirit.

Chapter 6

The people in the area had good reason to be afraid of the Mount St. Helens eruption. There have been many destructive volcanic eruptions around the world.

In the year 1691, Mount Vesuvius in Italy erupted and caused more than three thousand deaths. The famous Mount Etna on the island of Sicily erupted in 1729, killing at least twenty thousand people.

Mount Etna is still active to this day. In a recent eruption, the army was called in to set off bombs and build dams of earth. Using helicopters, they even dropped huge blocks of concrete. The idea was to make the lava flow in a different direction because a village was in its path. If the lava flow kept on its natural course, the village would be covered.

Even more shocking than these volcanoes was Krakatoa. The volcano Krakatoa is in Indonesia, a group of islands in the Pacific Ocean. In the year 1883, it exploded with terrible force. Most of the volcanic island was destroyed. A huge tidal wave developed as a result of the volcanic force. It killed thirty-six thousand people.

It is easy to see why people ran from Mount St. Helens when the smoke began to rise. We know what a volcano can do when it erupts. Old Harry Truman was the only one who thought he could live through it. And he probably thought this right up to the last minute.

The eruption of Mount St. Helens was less deadly than Vesuvius, Etna, or

Krakatoa because there were no towns or villages on its wilderness slopes. Only twenty-four people died and fifty-five were missing.

In ancient times, to be killed by a volcanic eruption was thought to be an act of the gods. Even the word volcano comes form the name of the Roman god, Vulcan. He was the god of fire. He was also the blacksmith to the gods, making their swords, chains, and armor. Vulcan's workshop was said to be underground, and each steaming volcano was thought of as one of his chimneys.

Not many people today believe in the Roman gods. But when Mount St. Helens exploded, the myth of Vulcan's power was there for all to see.

The Mount St. Helens eruption blew ash 60,000 feet in the air.

Chapter 7

It would be easy to think some god of fire had been at work. People who saw Mount St. Helens after the eruption could not believe their eyes. Many people came from places all around the world to look at the volcano's destruction.

Jimmy Carter, president of the United States at that time, flew over the area in an airplane on May 22, 1980. After his visit, he said, "It's the worst thing I have ever seen. It had been described to me earlier. But it was much worse than that."

The Mount St. Helens eruption was the most destructive in the history of the United States. President Carter talked about the first blast. The heat from the volcano reached eight hundred to a thousand degrees and burned everything to a distance of twelve miles. There was no escaping it.

The President spoke of the shock wave that came after the explosion, moving at the speed of sound—over seven hundred miles an hour. No one could survive the shock wave. Reid Blackburn found that out as he ducked down inside his car.

Finally there was the huge gush of rock and air mixed with blocks of ice. Once there were living things growing. Now there was nothing but a wasteland.

Sadly, old Harry Truman decided to stay in his lodge on Spirit Lake. He paid with his life for making that decision.

President Carter said the scene below his airplane was like the surface of the moon. The President had seen a lot of things in his lifetime, but the devastation of the Mount St. Helens eruption was in a class of its own.

The effects of the volcano could even be seen and photographed by weather satellites in space. These satellites have sensitive cameras that look at storms all over the world. The pictures they took of the United States at the time of the eruption showed a large black cloud moving to the east and getting bigger.

Chapter 8

The effects of the volcano were felt a long way off. Missoula, Montana, is four hundred miles away from Mount St. Helens. Sixty thousand people lived there at the time.

News about the early eruptions reached Missoula. The citizens read about it in their newspapers and they saw reports on television, but nobody worried very much about it. They felt they were far enough away to be safe.

On Sunday night, people in Missoula looked up at the sky after the big eruption. They saw a black cloud. It was coming from the west. It was not the kind of cloud they were used to: it was not a rain cloud.

30

They were looking at the cloud of ash from the Mount St. Helens explosion, carried along by the wind. Slowly, the cloud covered the city. And then the ash began to sift down like thick black snow. It settled on everything—streets, cars, porches, lawns.

There was something eerie about the way the ash came down. It was like a movie about an alien world. The particles just floated in and took over.

At the time, nobody knew if the ash was dangerous. Was it poisonous? Was it harmful if you breathed it into your lungs? What other problems might the black cloud bring? It had the odor of cement powder.

The city council took no chances. They issued a warning to the people: wear masks, and only travel if you really have to. All the schools closed; parents were asked to keep their children indoors.

The fall of ash was a shock to the

citizens in Missoula. They thought the volcano could not affect them. Still, they felt lucky when they saw what was happening to the people in Yakima, Washington, closer to the mountain. The ash was much deeper there, and more difficult to deal with.

People in Yakima had trouble driving because the ash in the air clogged their engines. Some of the police cars used a snorkel to filter the air.

It is estimated that sixty tons of ash fell out of the sky. In some places, it was six inches deep. Snow plows were used to clear the roads. Even after that, the mess remained for a long time.

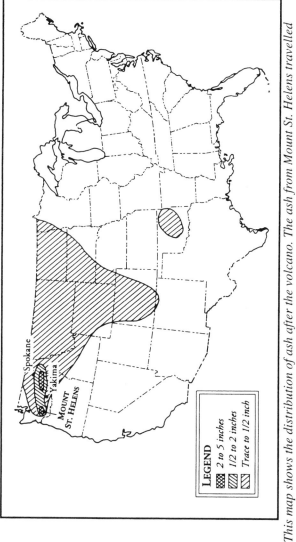

This map shows the distribution of ash after the volcano. The ash from Mount St. Helens travelled as far away as Oklahoma.

Chapter 9

Businesses were especially affected by the volcano. People did not go out to shop. They stayed home, away from the falling ash. Nobody was sure how dangerous the ash could be. The experience was new. This went on for days in some places.

Airports were closed. Trains stayed in the stations. Thousands of cars had to remain off the roads while plows worked to clear deep drifts of ash.

The men who worked the plows were used to moving snow in winter, but not deep ash in the month of May. More than six thousand miles of roads and state highways were closed just in the state of Washington.

Some roads were worse than others. A single state highway, which ran beside the Toutle River, sustained fifty million dollars in damage. Cars and trucks on this road were swept aside by the rush of mud.

Seven of the eight bridges over this highway were destroyed by mud slides. A long time passed and a lot of money was spent before these bridges were rebuilt.

The Toutle River and Cowlitz River flow down from Mount St. Helens and into the Columbia River. Between five and ten million yards of mud flowed into the Columbia. There was so much mud that the river shrank to only fourteen feet deep and two hundred feet wide, one-third its normal size. Thirty ocean-going ships were trapped in Portland, Oregon, and Vancouver, Washington. They could not move along the Columbia River until it was cleared of the excess mud.

In the state of Washington alone, 370,000 workers lost their jobs. Most of them did return to work, but around thirty-seven thousand of these jobs were gone forever.

Even though people's lives were disrupted, they kept their sense of humor. Some had fun with the plain white masks they wore over their mouth and nose to keep out the dust. The masks were similar to those that doctors wear when they perform operations. Some folks went around with lips and teeth painted on their masks.

In the state of Washington, they played games with the license plates on their cars. Some people used tape to cover the letter W, so the plate read "ashington."

Not everybody was laughing. Some people were angry. They wanted to know why there was not a better warning. Scientists had written for years that Mount St. Helens would erupt some day. Their reports described the event as it happened.

But they cannot predict when a volcano will erupt. If only that could be done! It would be fine if someone could announce: "Tomorrow at three o'clock in the afternoon, Mount St. Helens will erupt." When the early, small eruptions took place and there were earth tremors and steam, the scientists knew something was going to happen. But when? Tomorrow? Next week?

Warnings were given. Most people paid attention and left in time. The observers remained—those dedicated men at Coldwater One and Two. They stayed there to do their jobs.

And of course, there was Harry Truman. His case was different. He stayed because he was one of a kind. There was nothing anybody could say to make him leave.

Chapter 10

The winds that blow very high above Earth are called the jet stream. It is always in motion, although the path varies during the year.

The ash cloud from Mount St. Helens rose up sixty thousand feet into the jet stream, which carried it across the country. The ash then spread all the way around the world.

People saw bright red sunsets for a long time. They were caused by the sun's rays shining on the bits of dust high in the air.

It took some time for the volcano to quiet down. There were more than ten thousand small quakes on Mount St. Helens after the big one. For a couple of months, the volcano was quiet. But on October 16, 1980, there was another powerful eruption.

In January 1981, the mountain erupted again. But none of these events was as big as the main one in May. People were prepared now; they were watching and waiting. As a result, no great damage was done, and nobody was hurt.

No one will ever forget what happened to the wild animals when Mount St. Helens erupted. Nobody knows exactly how many were killed. The loss of animal life must have been heavy. People flying over the mountain in airplanes saw deer tracks in the ashes, so some did survive.

Try to imagine what it was like for the wildlife. They must have been very frightened when the eruption took place.

We can be sure that Harry Truman

loved all these creatures. He lived on the mountain for fifty years. They were like friends and neighbors to him.

The wild creatures may have sensed something was about to happen. They could feel the ground shake. They could hear the loud noises.

They had nowhere to go, but Harry Truman was not like them. He had a pretty good idea what might be coming. But he was too stubborn to leave. He was old; he had lived a full life. Maybe he decided that his life was going to be over soon, and this was the way he wanted it to end.

Chapter 11

How do eruptions happen? Where do volcanoes come from?

Our planet is made up of many layers of rock. The top layer is the crust. Molten rock called magma comes from very deep under the earth's crust. This crust is not all in one piece. It is in large slabs called plates. The plates move—but very slowly. A plate may move only half an inch a year, but its force is very strong. Nothing can stop it.

Two plates rubbing against each other will cause an earthquake. If there is a weak place between them, magma may burst through. This is the start of a volcano. We cannot see all the volcanoes that erupt. Some of them erupt under the ocean.

When magma comes out onto the surface, it is called lava. It may come through a vent that is already there because this is the easiest way out.

If a lot of magma boils up from the ocean floor, it will form a new island. Hawaii was formed this way.

Magma also makes mountains under the sea. There are mountain ranges under the oceans as big or bigger than those on land.

The process that forms volcanoes and islands under water is the same process that helps form earth. It is going on today, and it will continue to happen. It is a part of nature.

When Mount St. Helens erupted, there was a big explosion. Part of the top of the mountain blew up into the air. This does not happen with all volcanoes. Sometimes a crater or hole will open in the side of the mountain.

Then the lava comes flowing out through that hole.

Volcanoes are part of the natural way the planet is formed and changed. We travel miles to see beautiful mountains like Mount St. Helens or Mount Shasta, both part of the Cascade Range. Without volcanoes, these beautiful sights would not exist.

Just like the people who lived near the volcano, scientists have a sense of humor too. You'll see proof of it when you read about two domes named "Muffie" and "Domezilla."

The explosion that took place on May 18 blew the top off of Mount St. Helens, leaving a crater. Lava flowed from the crater and formed a dome. Later, the dome collapsed and another one formed.

It was not always easy to see the domes because of bad weather. As scientists flew past in airplanes, they could not get a good view.

The weather in Washington stayed bad for several weeks. But when the sky cleared on June 15, they were able to see a dome inside the crater. It was close to two hundred yards across and nearly forty yards high.

In July, new blasts occurred that caused the dome to collapse. Another dome formed where the old one had been. This process kept happening.

Muffie was observed in the middle of October. The dome was shaped like a steaming muffin that had just been taken from the oven.

Muffie did not last very long. It blew apart on December 13. In February, there were more earth tremors. This indicated that Mount St. Helens would be active again soon. Over February 5 to 7, a new dome grew. It was the biggest one so far. It grew the fastest, so they named it "Domezilla"—after the monster Godzilla of science fiction movies.

Mount St. Helens changes slowly in shape and size from forces deep inside Earth. Scientists know that the way Mount St. Helens looks today is not the way it will look in the future.

Chapter 12

We can learn something from Mount St. Helens. Earth has a life of its own. It goes on acting in its own way, and it will do so in the future. People should do their best to preserve the environment so Earth's changes cause as little damage as possible.

Before the eruption, Mount St. Helens was one of nature's magnificent sights. People came from miles away to see it and to camp on its slopes. They all found it an awesome sight. Eruptions over thousands of years created that beautiful mountain.

The Indians of the Pacific Northwest have their legends about Mount St. Helens. Now we have a modern legend to talk about. His name is Harry Truman. He was as strong and as willful as those ancient chiefs in his own way. He was a devoted old man who loved his mountain and his lake too much to leave them.

In 1982, the mountain and the surrounding area was named Mount St. Helens National Volcanic Monument. If you are lucky enough to visit there some day, think about Harry Truman. It is a lovely place once again. The trees have grown back. The rivers are flowing clean and filled with fish. There is beauty everywhere.

Bibliography

Bender, Lionel. *Volcano*. London: F. Watts, 1988.

Branley, Franklyn Mansfield. *Volcano*. New York: Corwell, 1985.

Bullard, Fred M. *Volcanoes of the Earth* (2nd rev. ed.). Austin: U of Texas Press, 1984.

Cas, Ray A. F., and John V. Wright. *Volcanic Succession, Modern and Ancient: A Geological Approach to Processes, Products and Successions.* London: Allen & Unwin, 1987.

Erickson, Jon. *Volcanoes and Earthquakes.* Blue Ridge Summit, PA: Tab, 1988.

Fodor, R. V. *Earth Afire!: Volcanoes and Their Activity.* New York: W. Morrow, 1981.

Goldner, Kathryn, and Carole Vogel. *Why Mount St. Helens Blew Its Top.* Minneapolis: Dillon, 1981.

Lauber, Patricia. *Volcano—The Eruption and Healing of Mt. St. Helens.* New York: Bradbury, 1988.

Ollier, Cliff. *Volcanoes.* Oxford: Basil Blackwell, 1988.

Palmer, Leonard, and KOIN-TV. *Mt. St. Helens: The Volcano Explodes!* Northwest Illustrated, 1980.

Place, Marian T. *Mount Saint Helens: A Sleeping Volcano Awakes.* New York: Dodd, Mead, 1981.

Poynter, Margaret. *Volcanoes; The Fiery Mountains.* New York: Messner, 1980.

Rosenfeld, Charles. *Earthfire: The Eruption of Mount St. Helens.* Cambridge, MA: MIT, 1982.

Simon, Seymour. *Volcanoes.* New York: Morrow Junior, 1988.

Wenkham, Robert. *The Edge of Fire: Volcano and Earthquake County in Western Northern America and Hawaii.* San Francisco: Sierra Club, 1987.